TRYING

TO GET

HOME

RAFAEL MAHDAVI

Printed by CreateSpace

An Amazon.com Company

Copyright© Rafael Mahdavi 2019

ISBN-9781674061948

FOUR PAINTINGS
Inspire
FOUR PAINTINGS

Preface............…....…..................................6

Texts and Paintings.....…..........………........7

Author Biography................................26

To Friendship

PREFACE

In many ways these four paintings are about my life-long quest, as a painter, to get home to America and Spain.

I have only spent eight of my seventy-three years in America but because of my mother who was from Kansas, I feel American. My father was Iranian but I have never been to Iran nor do I speak Persian. I feel Spanish too because I spent my formative years in Mallorca. I have also lived in England, Austria, Italy, Greece, and France but these countries didn't affect me the way Spain and America did.

Yet all in all and for what it's worth, I feel like an exile everywhere most of the time.

Rafael Mahdavi

LAS MENINAS
and
SHELF LIFE

In May 2017 I was in Madrid for a few days and I spent most of my time in the Prado. That's when I decided to do a painting about my life, based on *Las Meninas* by Diego Velázquez.

I first saw *Las Meninas* in 1956 when I was ten years old. I have seen it many times since then. I am not going to give you here one more analysis of this great painting with its enigmas and codes. Art critics, historians, and philosophers have already done this many times.

What triggered the idea to paint my life cycle, which I ended up calling *Shelf Life*, was the silhouetted figure of the man in a doorway in the background of *Las Meninas*, which takes place in Velázquez's Alcazar palace studio. In my own studio in Burgundy there is a door to the attic. In this doorway I envisioned the angel of death come to see me.

There are nine figures in *Las Meninas*. There is also the reflection of the king and queen in the background mirror, plus a dog. I decided to leave out the king and queen and two obscure figures in the background. The dog remained in my painting.

In the canvas I start my life cycle with me as the young man in the top left corner jumping into the painter's workspace. It is comparable to a leap of faith in myself.

The balding man, me, in the chair in the foreground drops his glass of water (a symbol of purity in classical painting) when he sees the angel of death in the doorway above his canvas nailed to the wall. The man in the chair sees himself stepping out from behind his canvas as if emerging from behind a theatre curtain.

Another *doppelgänger* cowers beneath the worktable on the right on which there is, among the paint cans and brushes, a clock indicating the hour close to midday or midnight.

In the foreground on the right stands a child, me, who looks at the viewer straight on. The small man with his back to the viewer in the lower left corner is holding a flashlight and looking for something on the studio floor.

Shelf Life, in the end, is about life and death.

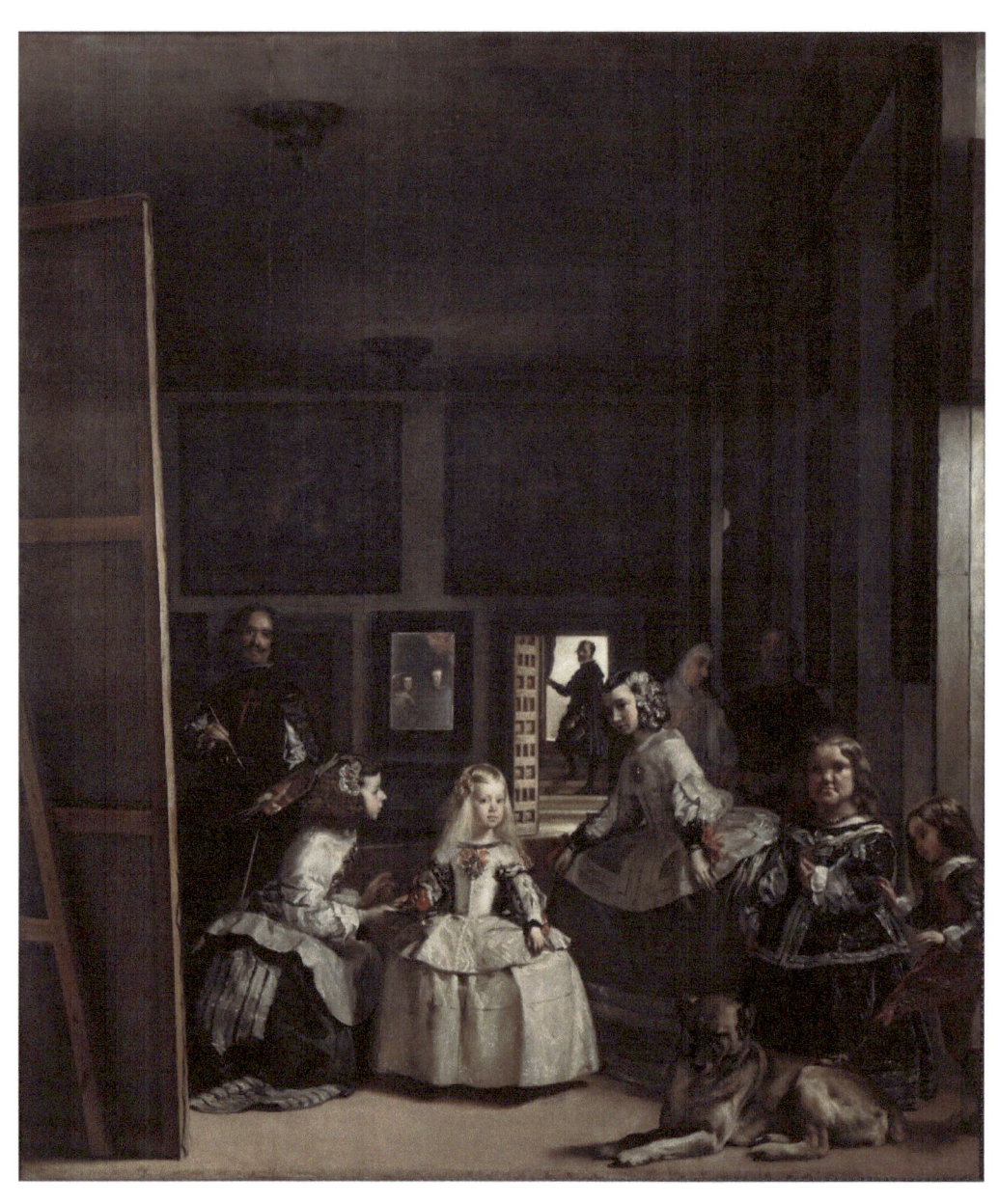

Las Meninas 1656

Diego Velazquez,

oil on canvas, 318 x 276 cm.

Prado Museum

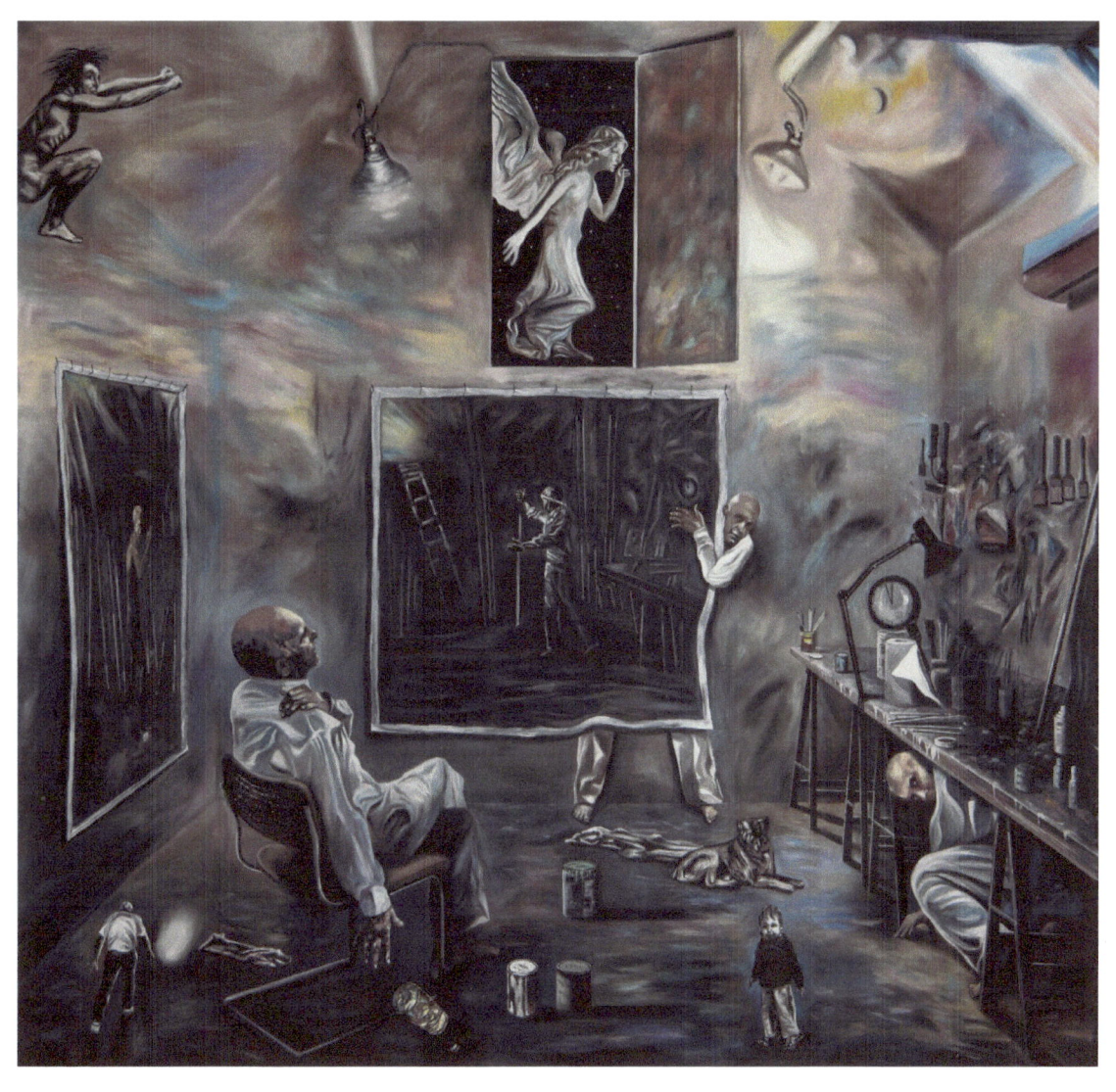

Shelf Life 2017

Rafael Mahdavi,

oil on canvas, 189 x 200 cm.

Private collection

GUERNICA

and

AMERICAN GUERNICA

I had not intended to paint another canvas based on a famous painting. But *Guernica* pushed its way to the fore of my consciousness one day as I reminisced about my childhood in Mallorca during the Franco era. In those days my friends and I never talked about which side our parents had taken in the civil war. The memory of the fratricidal war was ever-present. Many years later in 1975, I was in Madrid for a show of my paintings when Franco died. Soon after, Picasso's *Guernica* returned to Madrid from the Museum of Modern Art in New York City.

In May 2017 I saw Picasso's masterpiece at the Reina Sofia Museum. It remains for me, above all a work about war. Ever since my student days in the USA *Guernica* has been a shadowy presence in my life. I used to go look at it at the Museum of Modern Art in New York as often as I could. When I was about to finish art school I was drafted into the US Army. The Vietnam War and its televised horrors invaded our lives daily via television at the time. I fled to Paris and de facto became a draft dodger.

There are five people in Picasso's Guernica. One of them is only a head and an arm and is represented in my painting by a man in the upper right corner diving into the painting. Picasso's scene takes place in a room, hence the light bulb and the window. In my painting, titled *American Guernica*, I have placed my scene outdoors and painted a lantern in the sky and a window in the landscape. I have taken some liberties with the other four people and with the horse and bull.

The soldier in the foreground has my face.

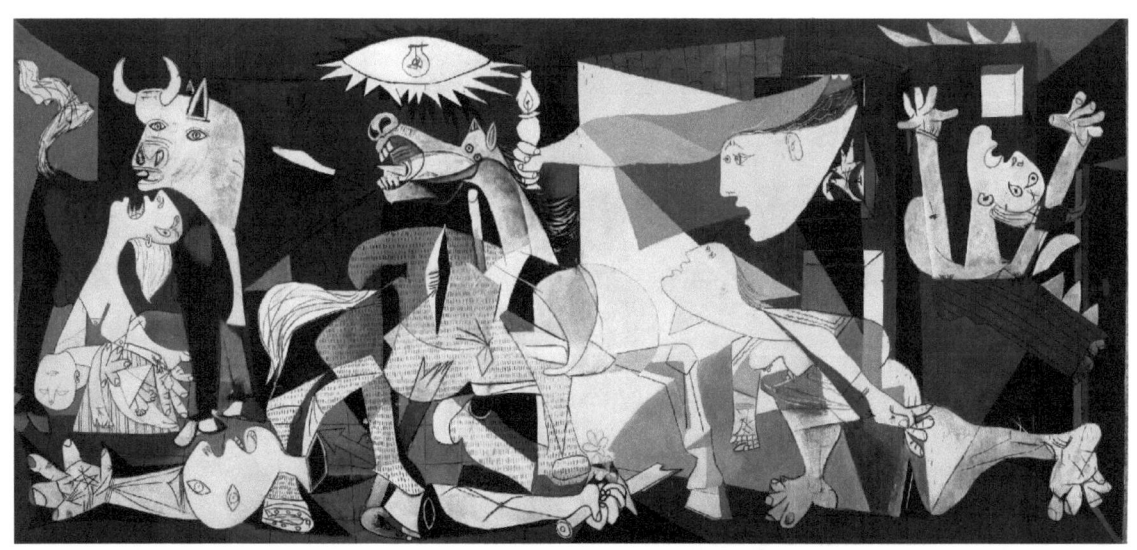

©succession Picasso 2019

Guernica 1937

Pablo Picasso,

oil on canvas 349 x 777 cm.

Reina Sofia Museum

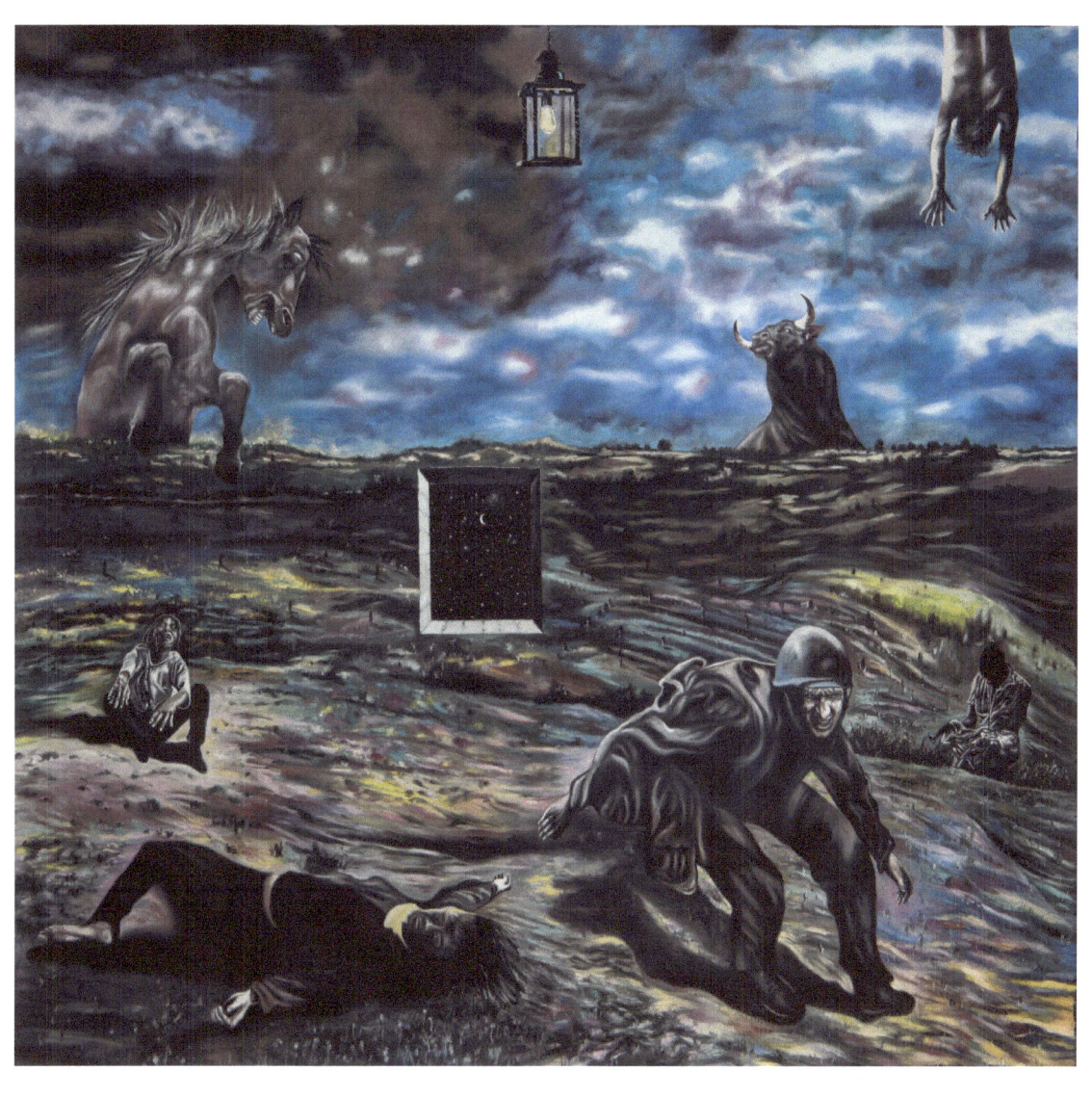

American Guernica 2018

Rafael Mahdavi

oil on canvas 189 x 200 cm.

Private collection

THE THIRD OF MAY

and

ONE DAY IN MAY

My painting *One Day In May* was inspired by Goya's *Third Of May,* and the title for my painting was suggested to me by Greg Light for three reasons: the title of Goya's work itself, I was born in May, and Greg wrote a play in 1979 called *One Day In May,* which was put on at the Edinburgh Festival and for which I did the stage sets.

As in *Shelf Life,* all the people in *One Day In May* are I, in different clothing. *One Day in May* is rich in possible interpretations. I only saw these meanings after friends pointed them out to me: three versions of me assassinating three versions of me.

Goya's work is about an assault on liberty.

The scene is set in my sculpture studio in Burgundy. Some of the tools hanging on the wall are potentially dangerous. Here in the studio, a powerful electrical spotlight replaces the square lamp in Goya's painting. The scene has a filmic quality and the steel beams and rods add a sense of hardness and brutality to the space. This is a place where creative hands are normally at work. Now the space is one for killing. The well-clad assassins stand in quasi-choreographic unison, their hands around their guns. The victims' arms and hands tell us about fear and resignation and defiance and fury.

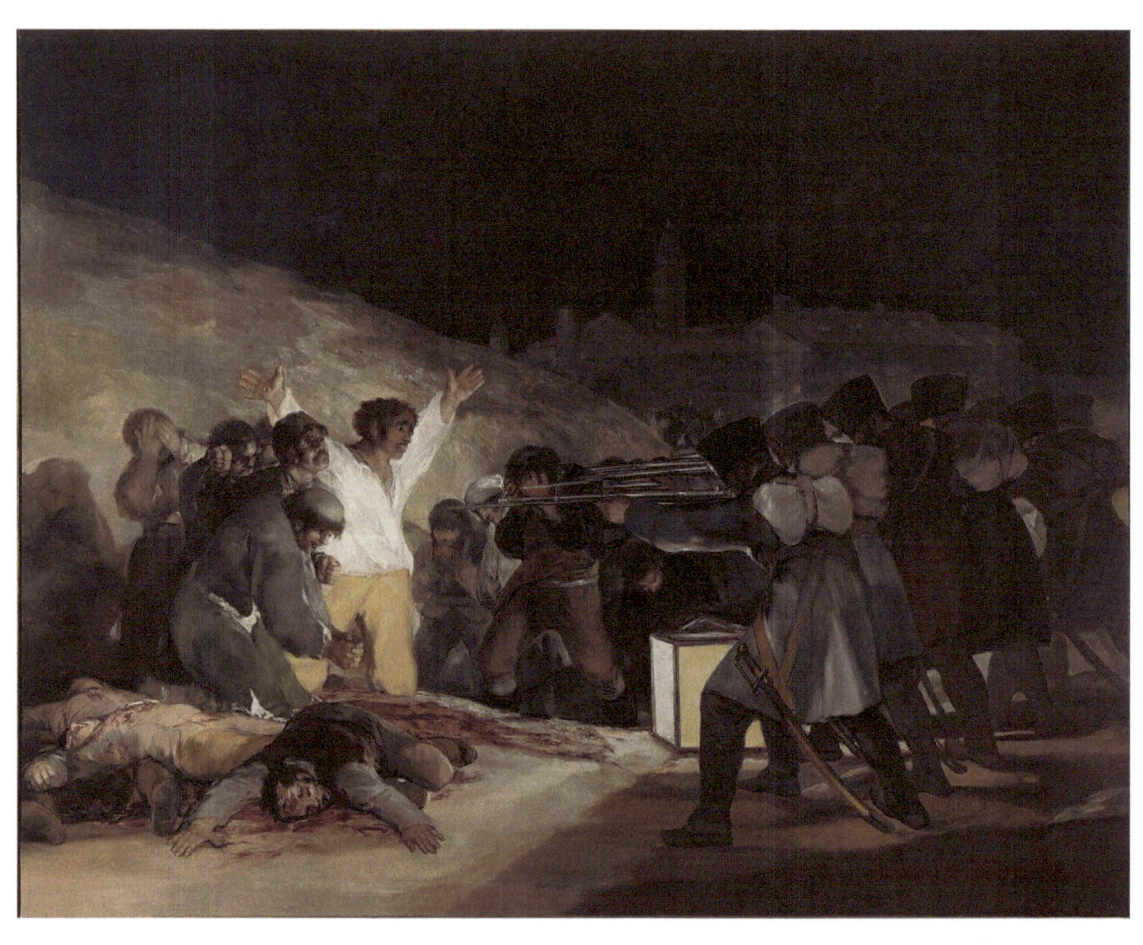

The Third Of May 1814

Francisco Goya

oil on canvas 347 x 268 cm

Prado Museum

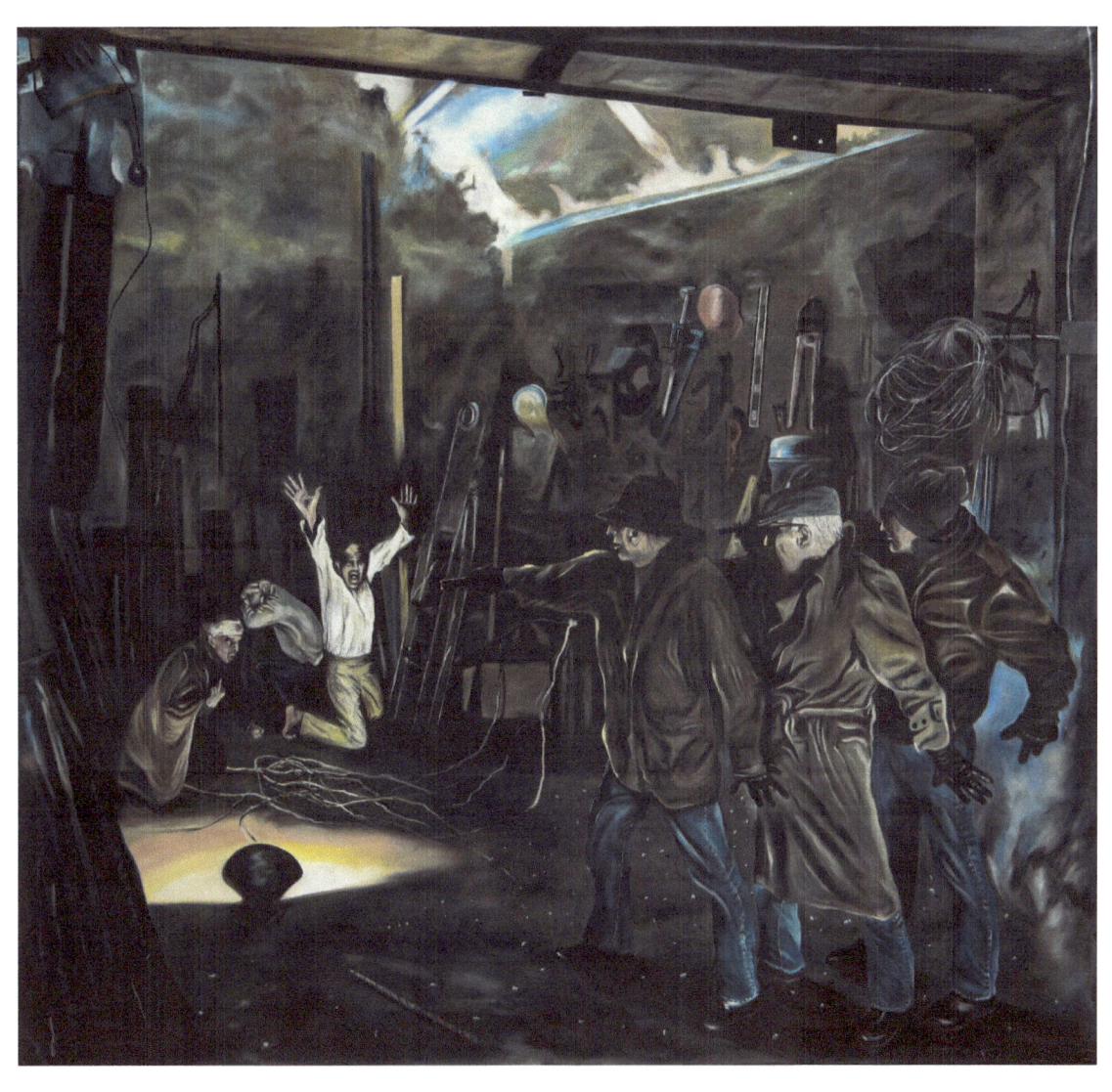

One Day In May 2018

Rafael Mahdavi

oil on canvas 189 x 200 cm.

Private collection

THE NIGHTHAWKS
and
INSPECTING ETERNITY

Inspecting Eternity is my take on Hopper's *The Nighthawks,* painted in 1942. The poet Rory Brennan gave me the title for this canvas. I had mentioned to him that whereas in Hopper's work the waiter behind the counter is the least important person, in my painting the waiter is the most important figure and he is looking at eternity in the sunset, not at the threesome at the table.

Maybe they are expats.

The bluish satellite dish on the upper right of my painting, which is present on my terrace in Burgundy, gives the setting here a slight science-fiction aura. Again in this painting, like in *Shelf Life* and *One Day In May*, all the characters are yours truly in disguise.

Hopper's painting always reminds me of my mother, who was a writer and lived in New York in the early nineteen forties. The diner in Hopper's painting was situated somewhere on Greenwich Avenue, not far from Sheridan Square where my Iranian father lived in the nineteen forties before he and my mother met, quit their jobs, and moved to Mazatlan in Mexico where my brother and I were born.

Hopper's diner painting, his vision of an American dusk, like much of his work, influenced Hollywood and Hollywood influenced how Americans and later of course Europeans saw America. The diner may not have served liquor but it has that silent and tough quality of some New York bars.

My painting takes place on an evening terrace in a sort of international landscape. Nothing makes much sense here: The sunglasses on the man's face at the center of the table, the laughter of the man at the far end of the table, and the woman with her back to us holding a cigarette. And in contrast to the casual dress and brittle nonchalance of the drinkers the servant bringing out a tray with a bottle of wine is well dressed, serious. And his eyes and thoughts are far away.

The canary in the foreground of my painting is a symbol. Well into the 20th century a caged canary was usually taken down into the coal mines; if the canary stopped singing it meant that the level of methane and carbon-monoxide was dangerously high and the miners should evacuate the tunnels as quickly as possible. In my painting, the canary is either flapping its wings in joy or because it is suffocating.

Finally, I have painted a barely decipherable skull in the woman's torn hat. I tend not to put too much stock in coincidences. But psychology has a way with the mind and at moments unexpectedly lays bare threads to the past, my past. My first canvas was a copy of a work by Thomas Sully, a nineteenth-century American painter. The painting's title was *The Torn Hat*.

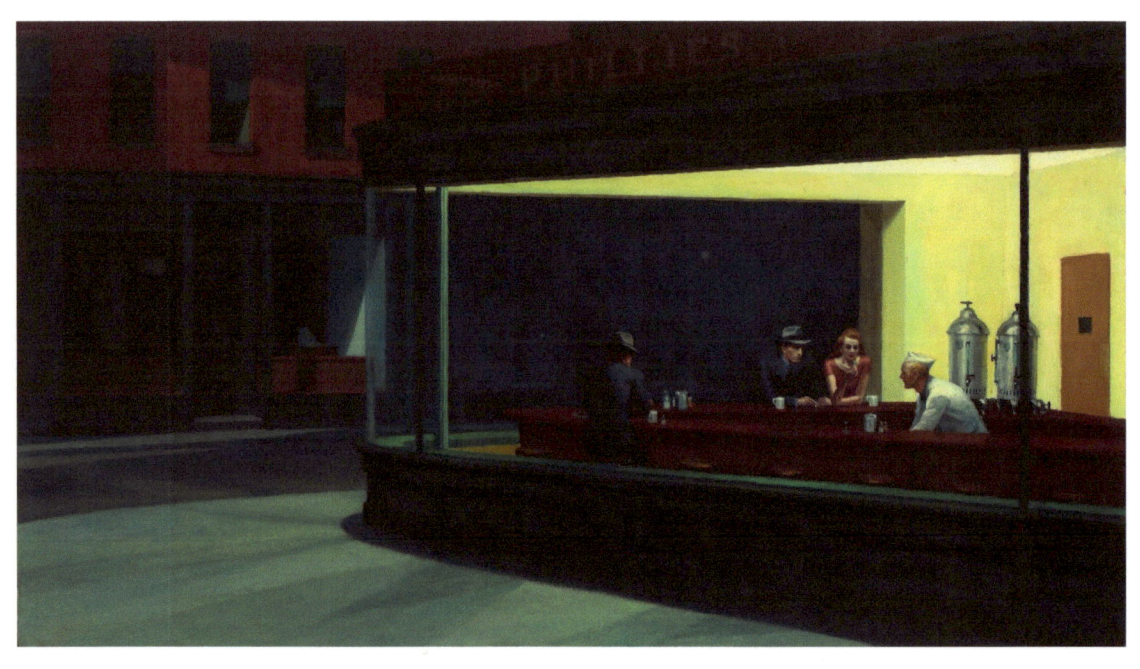

The Nighthawks **1942**

Edward Hopper

oil on canvas 84 x 152 cm.

Art Institute of Chicago

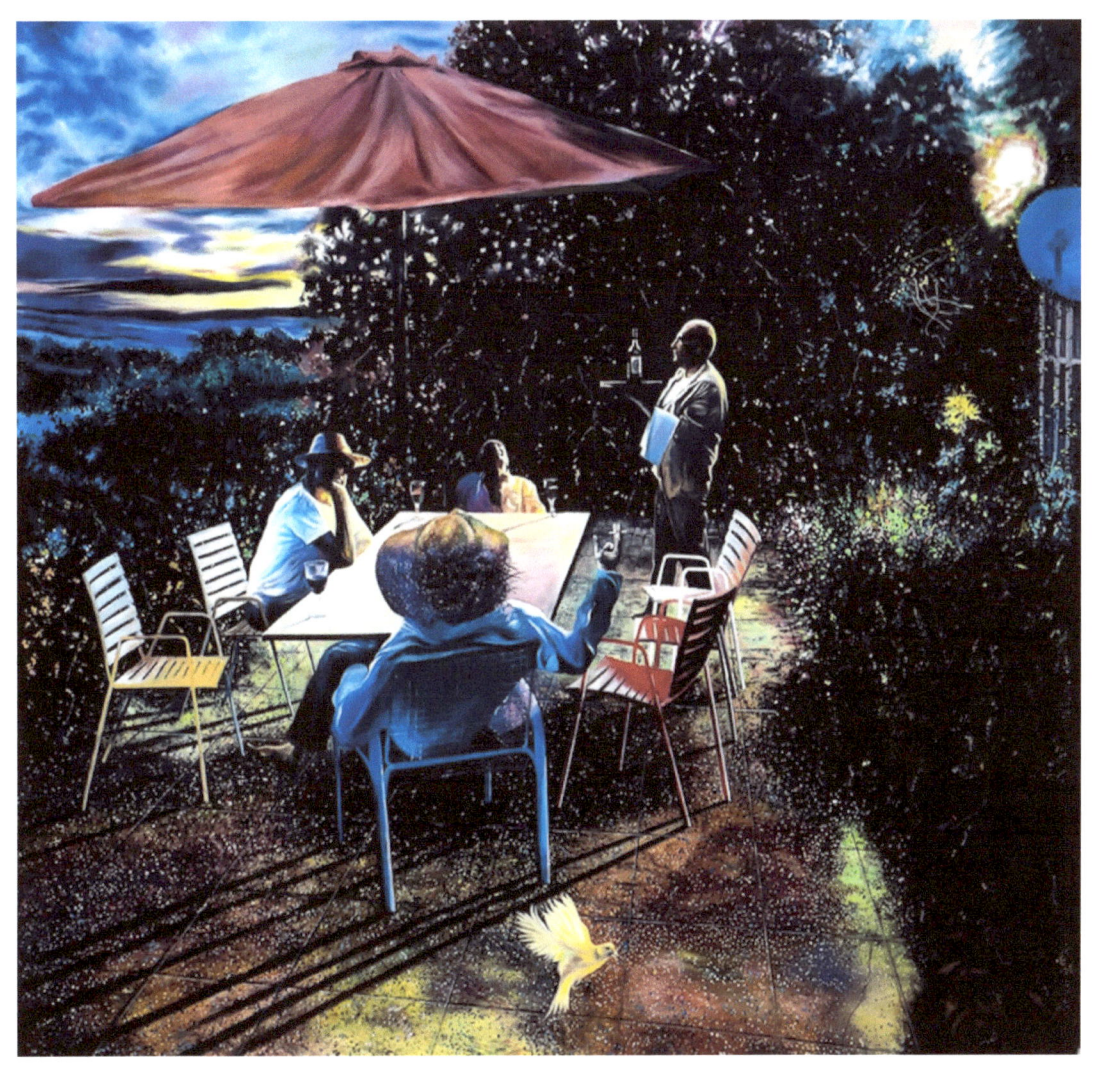

Inspecting Eternity 2018

Rafael Mahdavi

oil on canvas 189 x 200 cm

Private collection

Rafael Mahdavi was born in 1946. He attended European schools and completed his university studies in the United States. He speaks several languages and holds several passports. He divides his time between Burgundy and the Cycladic Islands.

www.rafaelmahdavi.com

www.ingramcontent.com/pod-product-compliance
Lightning Source LLC
Chambersburg PA
CBHW040058250526
45473CB00043B/1867